A GUIDE
TO
ELURA CAVE TEMPLES

A GUIDE
TO
ELURA CAVE TEMPLES

BY THE LATE

DR. JAMES BURGESS,
G.I.E., LL.D. F.R.S.E., ETC.

GYAN

Published by

GYAN

Gyan Publishing House
5, Ansari Road
Daryaganj, New Delhi-110002
Phone: 011-47034999, 9811692060
E-mail: books@gyanbooks.com

Distribution Network
gyanbooks.com
India, USA, Canada, UK, Australia, France

ISBN : 978-81-212-2551-9 (PB)
First Published, 1926

2nd Impression 2021

Printed at: Gyan Press, Delhi.

A Gruide to Elura Cave Temples
Author: Dr. James Burgess

A Guide
to
Elura Cave Temples

BY THE LATE

DR. JAMES BURGESS, C.I.E., LL.D., F.R.S.E., ETC.

REPRINTED BY
THE ARCHAEOLOGICAL DEPARTMENT
H. E. H. THE NIZAM'S GOVERNMENT

THE ROCK TEMPLES OF ELURA OR VELUR

CONTENTS

THE ROCK TEMPLES OF ELURA OR VERUL

LIST OF ILLUSTRATIONS

KAILASA: GENERAL VIEW [*Frontispiece.*

The Rock Temples
of
Elura or Verul

TEMPLES and monasteries fashioned out of the solid rock form a special feature among the early architectural remains of India. Of these there are probably forty or fifty groups in Western India, embracing as many as nine hundred or a thousand separate excavations. The majority of these rock-cut temples, as those at Ajanta, Kuda, Karle, Kanhairi, Junnar, Nasik, Bagh in Malva, and Aurangabad, are of Buddhist origin, but numbers also have been cut by the Brahmanical sects, both Saiva and Vaishnava. Elephanta, in the Bombay harbour, is one of the best known Saiva caves, but there are others at Jogesvari and Mandapesvara, in the island of Salsette; and at Badami, in the Kaladgi zilla, there is a group of three fine caves—one Saiva and two Vaishnava, with a small Jaina one. Jaina caves are few in number, but have been found also at Dharasimha, in the south-west of His Exalted Highness the Nizam's territory.

But of all the groups none are so deserving of notice as the large one at Elura (Lat. 20° 2′ N., Long. 74° 15′ E.), about fourteen miles north-west of Aurangabad, where are some of the largest and most elaborately carved specimens of the work of all three sects—Buddhists, Brahmans and Jains.

The Caves

The caves are excavated in the face of a hill, or rather the scarp of a large plateau, and run nearly north and south for about a mile and a quarter, the scarp at each end of this interval throwing out a horn towards the west. It is where the scarp at the south end begins to turn to the west that the earliest caves—a group of Bauddha ones—are situated; and in the north horn is the Indra Sabha or Jaina group, the other extremity of the series. The ascent of the ghat passes up the south side of Kailasa, the third of the Brahmanical group, and over the roof of the Das Avatara, the second of them. Sixteen caves lie to the south of Kailasa, and nearly as many to the north, but the latter are scattered over a greater distance.

Most of the caves have got distinguishing names from the local Brahmans, but it may be quite as convenient, for the sake of reference, to number them from south to north, beginning with the Bauddha caves, of which there are twelve, and passing through the Brahmanical series, of which seventeen are below the brow of the scarp, and a large number of smaller ones above, and ending with the Jaina ones, of which there are five at the extreme north. There are also some cells and a colossal Jaina image on the north side of the same spur in which is the Indra Sabha.

Buddhism

For the uninitiated it may be necessary to premise here that the earliest cultus of the Hindus of which we possess records was the Vedic,—so called from their most ancient books, the *Vedas*, and which was based on the worship of the elements and physical forces of Nature personified as divinities. Their favourite Gods were Indra, the God of the firmament, who gave rain and thundered; Agni, the God of fire and light; Varuna, of the waters; Ushas, the dawn; Vayu and the Maruts or winds; the Sun, addressed as Savitri, Surya, Vishnu; and other less distinctly defined objects of worship. The service of these Gods was at first probably simple enough, consisting of prayers, praises, libations, and sacrifices; but the priests soon elaborated the most complicated ritual probably ever invented, and of course, as in all rituals, they arrogated to themselves, through the proper performance of the ritual, powers not only superhuman, but even superdivine, compelling the Gods to their wills.

Among the aboriginal tribes, especially in Central and Southern India, as among many of the wild tribes to the present day, the worship of snakes, Bhutas or demons, and of a great undefined power, Siva or Mahadeva,—'the great God,'—seems to have prevailed, and probably many degenerate and semi-Aryans settled among these tribes soon learnt to believe in their superstitions.

The system of caste—an essential feature of Brahmanism—had become hard and fast, and was felt by some, especially among the lower castes, to be an undeserved yoke of iron. Men of all castes—often of very low ones—separated themselves from their kind, and lived lives of asceticism, despising caste as something beneath the consideration of a devotee, who was to rise by the merits of his own works and penances to a position where he might claim future felicity as a right. The Tirthakas and others, perhaps as early as the seventh century before Christ, threw aside all clothing, sat exposed to sun and rain on ant-hills or dunghills, or clothed in bark or in an antelope's hide, sought the recesses of forests and mountain peaks, to spend their days apart from the world and its vanities, and to win divine favour or become gods.

Gautama the Buddha was the son of the king of Kapilavastu, a small state in the north of Oudh, who at the age of twenty-nine forsook his palace with its pomp, his wife, and infant child, and became a devotee, sometimes associating with others of the class in their forest abodes in Behar, and sometimes wandering alone, seeking the solution of the mystery of existence, and unsatisfied with the dreamy conjectures of his teachers. After some six years, while engaged in a long and strict fast under a *pipal* tree near Gaya, wearied by exhaustion, like the North American Indian seers, he fell into a trance, when he attained to *Buddhi* or 'perfected knowledge,' and issued forth as the Buddha or 'enlightened,' the great teacher of the age. He is also called Sakya Muni, the

Muni or ascetic of the Sakya race; the Jina or 'vanquisher;' Sakhya Sinha, 'the lion of the Sakyas.' He celebrated this event in the stanzas—

> "Through various transmigrations
> Have I passed (without discovering)
> The builder I seek of the abode (of the passions),
> Painful are repeated births,
> Now, O house-builder! thou art found,
> No house shalt thou again build for me:
> Thy rafters are broken,
> Thy ridge pole is shattered,
> My mind is set at freedom (from outward objects),
> I have attained the extinction of desire."

With its dogma of metempsychosis Brahmanism discovered no final rest, no permanent peace; for to be born again, even in the highest heaven, was still to be under the empire of change, and consequently of further suffering in some still future birth. Hence it had created and fostered the thirst for final death or annihilation as the only escape from the whirlpool of miseries. To minister to this passion for extinction; to promulgate a new religious path for the deliverance of men from the endless series of transmigrations they had been taught it was their doom to pass through; to be the liberator of humanity from the impermanency, sorrow and unreality of existence, was the mission Sakya Muni, now at the age of thirty-five, set before himself as the proper work of a Buddha. His royal extraction, his commanding dignity and persuasive eloquence, the gentleness of his manners, his ardour and self-denying austerities, the high morality and the spirit of universal kindness that pervaded his teaching, fascinated the crowds, and he was soon able to send forth disciples, who had caught something of the fire of their master's enthusiasm, to propagate his doctrines. Caste he set aside: "My law," said Buddha, "is a law of grace for all." Belief in his doctrines and obedience to his precepts was, for Sudra and Dhed as for the Brahman, the only and the wide door to the order of the 'perfect.' And by the lower castes, whom the Brahmans had arbitrarily degraded and then superciliously despised, such teaching would be welcomed as a timely deliverance from the spiritual, intellectual, and social despotism of the higher castes.

Accompanied by his disciples he wandered about from place to place, principally in Gangetic India, subsisting on the offerings placed in his alms-bowl, or the provision afforded him by his wealthier converts, teaching men the emptiness and vanity of all sensible things, and pointing out the paths that led to *nirvana* or extinction—'the city of peace.' After forty-five years thus spent, Sakya Muni died in the north of Gorakhpur district, in Bengal. His disciples burnt his body and collected his relics, which were afterwards objects of worship.

Springing as it did from Brahmanism, of which it might be regarded as only a modification or one of its many sects or schools, Buddhism did not at first separate from Brahmanism so as to assume a position of hostility to it, or insult its divinities, or disparage its literature. It grew up slowly, and many of its most distinguished converts were Brahmans. Under the great emperor Asoka, about 260 B.C., it received the royal favour and patronage, and spread widely. The Bauddha traditions are full of the name of this king as the founder of temples, *viharas* or monasteries, *stupas* or commemorative domes, asylums, and other edifices. His son Mahendra and his daughter Saughamitra became devotees, and missions were sent out to all parts of India, to Ceylon, Kashmir, Afghanistan, etc.

The Bauddha religion flourished and spread for centuries. Chinese travellers came to India to visit the spots associated with the founder's memory, to learn its laws, and carry away the books containing its teachings. In the seventh century of our era it had begun to decline; in the eighth it was apparently rapidly disappearing, and shortly after became almost extinct in India, though it lingered about Benares, and perhaps about Bahroch, till the eleventh century. It has been thought that it was extinguished by Brahmanical persecution; but the evidence is not sufficient to establish this. It probably died out through the ignorance of its priests and the corruption of its doctrines, the descendants of its followers becoming merged among the Jains, whose teachings and ritual are very similar, or falling into the surrounding Hinduism of the masses. It probably never was the predominant religion in India, and alongside it, during its whole existence, Saivism continued to flourish and hold, as it does still, the majority of the lower castes.

It was the Buddhists who first carved rock temples and monasteries. The earlier ones are very plain; a square hall with cells at the back and sides for monks, and an arched or flat-roofed cave, often with a circular apse at the back around a *dahgoba* for worship, were the usual forms. The dahgoba is a low thick cylinder supporting a hemispherical dome surmounted by a square capital, and was meant to represent the monument built to enshrine a bone or other relic of Buddha. Relics, however, were probably placed *upon* the capital of the dahgoba, which was almost always covered by a wooden umbrella. Little sculpture was at first employed in any of these works, for Buddha did not preach idol-worship : but in course of time his own image came to be worshipped, and to be repeated in all parts of the caves, and still later other beings were associated with him as objects of worship : until in Nipal at the present day the Bauddha pantheon is a very extensive one.

We shall now begin at the south end of the series of the Elura caves.

Cave I

The first few Buddha caves are popularly known as the Dhedavada, or low castes' quarter ; and though Dr. J. Wilson supposed this might have originated as a nickname given in sarcasm by the Brahmans, and from similarity of sound, to 'Theravada,' or the quarter of the *Theros* or Bauddha priests, yet—as probably in a majority of cases the Buddha converts were made from Dhedas and other partially aboriginal low-caste tribes—the name of Dhedavada may have been quite correctly applicable to the Bauddha series of caves from the first. Or, as the caves have evidently been inhabited long after they ceased to be used for religious purposes, these may have been appropriated by Dheds.

The first cave is not of great interest, except as perhaps one of the oldest caves here, and probably attached to the next cave. It was a vihara or monastery with eight cells inside for monks, four in the back and four in the south side. It is 41 feet 6 inches wide and 42 feet 3 inches deep. The front has all fallen except one pillar near the south end, and probably belonged to the next cave. Outside, in what may have been the south end of verandah, is another cell or room.

CAVE II

The next is a large and interesting cave. It was doubtless a chapel or hall for worship. It is approached by a flight of steps leading to the top of a stylobate, the front of which has been carved in compartments with fat *ganas* or dwarf figures, often in grotesque attitudes. On this, four pillars with pilasters at the ends, once supported the roof of the verandah, but this is now entirely gone. At the north end of the verandah is a fat squatting figure with a high and elaborate head-dress or *mukut*, a jewelled cord over his breast, and a bouquet of flowers in his right hand, attended by a *chauri*-bearer with his fly-flap. Right and left are small figures of Buddha sitting, with attendant *chauri*-bearers. On the south was probably a similar female figure, but only the attendant is left, and a *gandharva* or cherub holding a garland over her head. These figures are often met with, and may be conventional representations of the prince who executed the cave, and his wife, or possibly of Sakra or Indra,—a favourite divinity with the Bauddhas and Jains, and represented as almost a servant or attendant on the Jina,—with his wife Indrani.

Two tall guardians or *dvarapalas* stand by the door with lofty head-dresses and aureoles, *gandharvas* or cherubs over their shoulders, and a female figure with an aureole or nimbus behind her head, standing between the *dvarapala* and the door.

The front wall is pierced by a door and two windows, and much of the remaining wall, together with the jambs of the windows, is covered with sculptures of Buddha. The cave has lateral galleries along each side, and, exclusive of these, measures nearly 48 feet square. The roof is supported by twelve massive columns arranged in a square, with elegant cushion capitals and high square bases, standing on a platform raised about 18 inches above the front and side aisles, which are about 17 feet high. Except the four in the back row, they have little dwarf figures on the upper corners of the square portions of the shafts; above these they are circular and fluted, while the spaces between the dwarf figures and a belt below them are covered with rich and varied arabesques.

The side galleries have each four pillars in front, of a different design, while the fronts of the galleries are carved with florid work and musicians. In the five compartments of the back of each are as many seated Buddhas, each in the same attitude as the colossal one in the shrine, and with his usual *chauri*-bearers, the one on his right hand usually holding also a lotus-bud. These side galleries were perhaps an afterthought, for that on the south has been cut into the roof of Cave I. in some places, and in that on the north some of the figures are quite unfinished.

The *dvarapalas* of the shrine are large figures 13 to 14 feet high : that on the left or north side is very plainly dressed with his robe fastened round the waist by a string, his head-dress is the *jata* of plaited hair worn by ascetics ; he has a small image of Amitabha Buddha as a crest on the front of it, and holds a *mala* or rosary in his right hand and a lotus stalk in his left. The other (on the south side) as is almost always the case, has a very richly jewelled head-dress, with a small dahgoba on the front of it, bracelets, armlets, a thick jewelled Brahmanical cord or *janvi* ; and a small bouquet of flowers in his right hand. Both are attended by two pairs of flying *gandharvas* above, while about midway up the wall are others with curly wigs and bearing garlands. Between each *dvarapala* and the door is a female with a flower in her right hand.

The shrine contains a colossal Buddha seated on a throne borne up at the corners by lions, and hence called a *sinhasana*. His feet rest on a nearly circular plinth ; with the thumb and forefinger of his right hand he grasps the little finger of his left, through the palm of which passes the corner of his robe. This attitude, as well as a few others, are repeated scores of times, and, as it is that of the Teacher enumerating, like Socrates, the points of his argument or lecture on his fingers we may appropriately style it the teaching attitude. His head, always represented as covered with small knobs as of short-cut curly or woolly hair, and a with a pile of them on the top, is surrounded by the usual nimbus. On each side of it are *gandharvas*. At each end of his throne stand his attendant *chauri*-bearers, who are just the duplicates of the warders outside. And on each side wall is a colossal standing figure of a Buddha, or perhaps a Bodhisatva,—a being in the course of preparation for being born as a Buddha in a future birth. His right hand hangs down and has the palm turned out, the left is bent upwards and holds a part of his robe. In the corners next to these two figures are four worshipping figures, one above the other. This cell is dark, but one of the least damaged of the sort here.

On each side of the shrine is a double cell in line with the side aisles. In the outer of these and all over the front wall are many figures of Buddha in different attitudes, with his attendants, the largest figure, however, being of a female right opposite to the north *dvarapala* of the shrine and with similar head-dress, lotus, etc., attended by two smaller females with lotus flowers. It is difficult to say whom the principal figure here may represent. It may be Maya the mother of Buddha, or Yasodhara his wife, or a female counterpart of Avalokitesvara or Padmapani, the Bodhisatva of the divine Buddha Amitabha, all of whose symbols she possesses. In other places, too, we find Padmapani attended by a female, and frequently by two.

The horse-shoe-shaped arch, representing the window of a *chaitya*, the Buddhist rail pattern, and the dahgoba in bas-relief, which are almost the sole ornaments in the early Bauddha caves at Bhaja, Bedsa, Kondane, and Nasik, have in this and in the other caves here almost entirely disappeared; we find only two small dahgobas over an image of Buddha in the cell on the south of the shrine, and a third on the end of the south gallery. This and the profusion of imagery would seem to indicate a late date for the cave. Moreover, though evidently intended, like the chaitya caves, solely as a place for worship, it has not the arched roof so general in such caves. It is very difficult to fix an age for it, but it may have been begun in the third or fourth century, while the carving may have been continued down to the sixth or seventh.

Cave III

Returning northwards, between the last cave and the third is a cistern now filled up with earth. This was an indispensable adjunct of all cave temples in India.

Cave III, somewhat lower down in the rock, is a vihara or monastery, and belongs to about the same period as Cave II : possibly it is the older of the two, but, like it, never seems to have been perfectly completed. The south half of the front wall is now entirely gone, as is also the verandah before it. It measures nearly 46 feet square and about 11 high, the roof being supported by twelve square columns with drooping ears falling over circular necks,—a sort of Indian Ionic. Three of them on each side are only blocked out, with octagonal necks. The cells for the monks have been twelve,—five on each side and two in the back,—but the front one on the south side is now broken away. Between the two cells in the back is the shrine,—smaller than in the last cave, and the figures more abraded, but otherwise almost exactly the same ; the uppermost of the four supplicants in the corners, however, has no attendants

CAVE III

On the north wall of the cave are two small sculptures on e of them just begun) of Buddha and attendant *chauri*-bearers.

There is a window in the front wall, north of the door, which has been divided by two colonnettes, both broken. It is bordered outside by a neat florid pattern. In the north end of the verandah was a chapel, which still remains. It contains a Buddha with his legs crossed in front, and, as usual in most of the Elura caves, holding or touching the little finger of his left hand with the forefinger and thumb of his right. He is seated on a lotus, the stalk of which is supported by small figures having snake or *naga* hoods over their heads,—the males usually with three, five, or seven hoods, and the females with one or three. This sort of seat is known as a *padmasana*, or lotus-throne. Buddha is attended, as usual, with two *chauri*-bearers, the one on his left having a *jata* or head-dress of plaited hair, with long locks hanging over the front of his shoulders, and a lotus in his left hand. Above their heads are *gandharvas*, or Hindu cherubs.

The Buddhists worship the images of their sage upon this principle:—they believe that the act is in itself an *opus operatum;* that as the seed germinates when it is put into the earth, without any consciousness upon the part of the elements relative to the vivifying influence they exercise, so does merit arise from the worship of the images of Buddha, though the being they represent is unconscious of the deed. And this merit is, in like manner, spontaneously, without the intervention of any intelligent agent, productive of prosperity and peace. For the same reason they worship the *bo*-tree, under which he attained to Buddha-hood, and the relics of the sage and of his disciples enshrined in dahgobas, etc.

To the spectator's right hand is a rude carving that might readily be passed over, but which is of some interest. It may be called a Bauddha Litany, and occurs elsewhere in the caves of the sect, as on the verandah wall of Cave IV at Ajanta, at Kanheri, and in a very complete form in Cave VII, one of the second group at Aurangabad. Avalokitesvara or Padmapani is represented in the middle with four small scenes on each side. The uppermost on his right represents a great fire with a figure praying towards Padmapani; the second, a figure with a sword, and his intended victim in a similar beseeching attitude; the third and fourth on this side are broken, but represented captives, and persons in a ship praying for deliverance from their threatened fates. On his left again we have, first, a praying figure with a lion behind it; second, another with two snakes; third, with an enraged elephant; and fourth, Kali, the Goddess of death, pursuing the victim who prays the 'good lord' for deliverance. This stone Prayer may almost be read in the words of the Church prayer-book.

Cave IV

The next four or five caves are somewhat difficult to arrange satisfactorily; indeed it is not easy to say how many of the apartments were separate caves, or how many belonged to one. We shall, however, take first the lower floor of the next group as Cave IV. It is much ruined, the whole of the outer half of it having disappeared. It measured 35 feet wide by 39 deep up to two pillars and pilasters with capitals having drooping florid ears, the shafts being square below, and the necks having 32 flat flutes, behind which is a cross aisle. At the left or north end of it is a prominent figure of Padmapani seated like Buddha, with high *jata* head-dress, a small image of Buddha as a crest on the front of it, and his locks hanging down upon his shoulders, a deer-skin over his left shoulder, a *mala* or rosary in his right hand, and clasping a lotus to his left thigh. He is attended by two females, one on his right hand with a rosary, the other holding a flower-bud. Above the first is a standing Buddha or Bodhisatva; and over the latter Buddha, seated cross-legged on a lotus with his right hand raised and the left down.

The back wall is pierced with doors to two cells and the shrine. The *dvarapalas* are carved with elaborate head-dresses, and a dwarf stands between each and the door. In the shrine Buddha is seated in the usual teaching attitude with a nimbus behind his head and the foliage of the sacred *Bo*-tree rising from behind it. The *chauri*-bearers in this case stand *behind* the throne, and are carved in *bas-relief*. The tall attendant on his left is richly dressed, and wears a jewelled cord like the Brahmanical *janvi* across his breast : the other is destroyed.

In a cell on the south side of this cave is some sculpture. The west side is broken away, and is now blocked up by a mass of rock that has slipped down from above. The figures are principally Buddha with attendants, and a female with rosary, etc.; but to the west of the door is a Padmapani, and half of what has been already described in the last cave as a sort of litany, only that there are two supplicants in each case, and that a smaller flying figure of Padmapani is represented before each group.

Cave V—Maharwada

Ascending a few steps we enter a very large vihara about 117 feet deep by 58½ wide, exclusive of two large side recesses, the roof being supported by twenty-four pillars with square shafts, and capitals of type found at Elephanta and in Cave II here, having a thick compressed cushion as the chief feature of the capital. They are arranged in two rows of ten each from front to back, and the space between is divided into three passages by two low stone benches. As the cave had at least twenty cells for monks these were probably either the low tables of their refectory ; or it may possibly have been a sort of monastic school, and these benches, the reading-desks of the scholars ; or it may have been that they served both purposes in turn.

At the entrance of the left aisle is a chapel which contained a sitting figure of Buddha, now quite destroyed. In the shrine at the back is a large seated Buddha with attendants, and on each side the door in arched recesses are attendants separately; Padmapani, on the north side, attended by two small female figures with head-dresses resembling royal crowns. The other figure is more richly bejewelled and similarly attended, while *gandharvas* or cherubs on clouds above bring garlands and presents to them.

Connected with this cave on the south side was another shrine, over Cave IV, but the rock has fallen away, so that it is inaccessible without a ladder. This shrine contained the usual image of Buddha and attendants; also a female figure holding a lotus-stalk, with her attendants. Round it was a passage or *pradakshina* for circumambulation, as in Hindu temples. From this passage and the vestibule in front several cells were entered. The half of the shrine, however, has slid down, and now blocks the west side of the front cell of Cave IV just below it.

Cave VI

Proceeding northwards we enter a hall with a stair-landing in it from the cave below. This hall, of which the west side is entirely gone, is 26 feet from north to south and 28¾ from east to west. On the east side it has three cells, and on the north has been separated from a still larger and very lofty hall by two pillars and their corresponding pilasters, of which only one pillar and pilaster remain. The central hall was 26½ feet wide and about 43 feet in length, exclusive of the ante-chamber at its east end, cut off from it by two pillars and their pilasters, as was another hall on the north, 27 feet by 29, similar to that on the south, with three cells in the back, and as many in the east end, all with very high steps.

The ante-chamber in the front of the shrine is filled with sculpture. On the north end is a female dressed exactly in the garb of Padmapani, who is the gigantic *dvarapala* on the north side of the shrine door. On the south end is a similar female figure with a peacock at her left hand ; below it a pandit reading. This is supposed to represent Sarasvati, the Goddess of learning. The *dvarapalas* are tall and carefully cut, with foliage over their heads and attendants beside them. A female stands between each and the door. The door is lofty and boldly cut.

In the shrine is a large image of Buddha seated, with the usual attendants. On the side walls are three rows, containing each three Buddhas with their feet turned up while below them on each side are worshippers and others.

On the north side of the front hall a passage divided from a balcony or small cave by two pillars is the only way of access now left to a shrine which I would be disposed to call

Cave IX

This has a well-carved facade as seen from the south, which it faces. It consists of a small outer balcony and an inner covered portico, separated by two pillars, square below, octagonal above, and with drooping-eared capitals. On the back wall are two deep pilasters with the compressed cushion capitals of the Elephanta cave style. These divide the wall into three compartments : in the centre one is a seated Buddha with four *gandharvas* above ; in the left one is Padmapani with female attendants and two fat *gandharvas* above ; in the east one is Buddha's other usual attendant with two females, etc.

Cave VII

Returning now through Cave VI to the stair, we descend into a large plain vihara 51½ feet wide by 43½ deep, the roof supported by only four square columns. It has five cells in the back, and three on each side. It is noways interesting, and appears never to have been finished.

Cave VIII

This may be entered from the last by a roughly cut passage, or perhaps unfinished cell, in its north wall, and may be described as consisting of two rooms and the shrine, with its circumambulatory passage. The inner hall is 28 feet by 25, with three cells on the north side, and is cut off by two pillars and pilasters at each end,—on the east from the shrine, with its surrounding *pradakshina* and on the west from the outer apartment.

The shrine has the usual *dvarapalas* and their attendants at the door; and inside is the seated Buddha with his attendants, but in this case Padmapani has *four* arms, holding the *chauri* and the lotus in his left hands, and over his shoulder hangs a deer-skin. At his feet are small figures of devotees, and behind them is a tall female figure with a flower in her left hand, and a *gandharva* over her head. The other tall male attendant has a similar companion on his left, with a lotus flower and a rosary in her hands.

On the wall, at the south entrance to the *pradakshina*, is a sculpture of Sarasvati, somewhat similar to the one in the cave above. Opposite is a cell, and in the passage two more, while behind the shrine is a long raised recess with two square pillars in front.

The outer room is 28 feet by 17, with a slightly raised platform filling the west end of it. On the north side is a chapel on a raised floor with two slender columns in front, on the back wall of which is a seated Buddha with attendants dressed nearly alike, with Brahmanical cords, necklaces and armlets, but no chauris,—the one on Buddha's left holding in his hand a three-pronged object, which is half of what we shall find as his frequent cognizance in other caves,—the *vajra* or thunderbolt; hence he may be styled Vajrapani. On the west wall is Padmapani with the female figure that we find so frequently associated with him.

Coming out of this by the large opening on the south side, just under Cave IX, we find on the face of the rock to the west, but partly broken away, a sculptured group of a fat male and female, the latter with a child on her knees and attendant. This group occurs also at Ajanta and Aurangabad, but whether meant to represent the patron of the Bauddhas when the cave was excavated, or the prince who excavated them, with his queen, or some other mythical group, it is not easy to say.

There is now a break in the continuity of the caves, and we have to go some way northwards to

Cave X—Visvakarma

This is the only chaitya cave here,—the cathedral temple of the Bauddha caves. And, though not so magnificent in its proportions, or severe in its decoration, as the great cave at Karle, it is still a splendid work, with a large open court in front surrounded by a corridor, the frieze above its pillars carved with representations of the chase, etc. The inner temple, consisting of central nave and side aisles, measures 85 feet 10 inches by 43, and 34 feet high. The nave is separated from the aisles by twenty-eight octagonal pillars 14 feet high, with plain bracket capitals, while two more square ones just inside the entrance support the gallery above and cut off the front aisle. The remote end of the nave is nearly filled by a huge dahgoba, 15½ feet in diameter, and nearly 27 feet high, which, instead of consisting of a simple circular base surmounted by a hemispherical dome and square capital, as in all the older examples, has in this case a large frontispiece nearly 17 feet high attached to it, on which is a colossal seated figure of Buddha, 11 feet high, with his feet down, and his usual attendants, while on the arch over his head is carved his Bo-tree, with *gandharvas* on each side.

The arched roof is carved in imitation of wooden ribs, each rising from behind a little Naga bust,—alternately male and female,—and joining a ridge piece above. The triforium or deep frieze above the pillars is divided into two belts, the lower and narrower carved with crowds of fat little gambolling figures (*ganas*) in all attitudes. The upper is much deeper, and is divided over each pillar so as to form compartments, each containing usually Buddha with two attendants and two Bodhisatvas. The inner side of the gallery is also divided into three compartments filled with figures.

At the ends of the front corridor are two cells and two chapels with the usual Bauddha figures repeated. From the west end of the north corridor a stair ascends to the gallery above, which consists of an outer one over the corridor and an inner one over the front aisle, separated by the two pillars that divide the lower portion of the great window into three lights : for it is not, as at Karle, Ajanta, and elsewhere, a single open horse-shoe arch here. From the outer area, too, small chapels are entered, each containing sculptures of Bauddha mythology, and where the very elaborate head-dresses of the females of that period may be studied. Over the chapel to the right of the window is a remarkable group of fat little figures (*ganas*), and the projecting frieze that crowns the facade is elaborately sculptured with pairs of figures in compartments. This cave is locally known as the *Sutar's jhopra*, or Visvakarma, and is much frequented by carpenters, who come to worship the image of Buddha as Visvakarma, the patron of their craft.

High up on each side are two small chapels, difficult of access, and not specially interesting.

Cave XI—The Do Thal

A little further north is the cave known as *Do Thal*, because it has been for long regarded as consisting only of *two* stories. In 1876 the excavation of the earth from what was then the lower floor revealed the landing of a stair from a cave below. This was partially excavated in 1877, and revealed a verandah 102 feet in length by 9 wide with two cells and a shrine behind in which is Buddha with Padmapani and Vajrapani as his attendants, the latter with the *vajra* in his right hand.

The stair leads into a similar verandah above, with eight square pillars in front, the back wall pierced with five doors. The first, at the stair-landing, is only the commencement of a cell. The second, to the south, leads into a shrine with a colossal Buddha, his right hand on his knee, and the left in his lap. In front of the throne, rising from the floor, is a small female figure holding up a water-jar, and to the right another sitting on a prostrate figure. Buddha's left hand attendant has a flower-stalk by his left side, and over the bud is a *vajra* or thunderbolt—a short object with three prongs on either end. On the same (or right) wall are three other tall standing males. The one next Vajrapani has a similar flower-stalk supporting an oblong object which strongly resembles a native book tied up with a string. The next holds a lotus-bud, and the last a pennon. On the return of the wall is a tall female figure with a flower. On the north side are also three figures, one of which holds a very long sword; and on the return of the wall on this side a fat male figure, adorned with garlands and necklaces, with a round object (cocoanut ?) in his right, and perhaps a money-bag in his left—possibly meant to represent the excavator. Above these figures on either side are seven figures of Buddhas, the foliage of the peculiar Bo-tree of each extending over his head like an umbrella. The central door leads into a small hall with two square pillars, and partially lighted by two small windows. Behind it is a shrine with a Buddha on a *sinhasana*, or throne supported by lions; his feet crossed in front of him, his right hand hanging over his knee. Vajrapani here holds up his *vajra* in his right hand.

The fourth door has a carved architrave and leads into a shrine very similar to the corresponding one on the other side the central area. Buddha, as usual, with his attendants Padmapani, bejewelled and wearing a thick cord or necklace, and Vajrapani, with three tall figures on either side, the one next to Vajrapani having a book on the top of the flower-bud he holds, the strings by which it is held together being distinctly visible. There are seven squatting Buddhas above, with the foliage extending over their heads; and on the inside of the front wall, on the north, a fat male figure with garlands and necklaces, a round object,—perhaps a cocoanut—in his right hand, and in his left what appears to be a purse from which coins are dropping out. On the south side stands a female with a flower in her left hand. These possibly represent the patron and patroness of the cave. The last door leads into a cell.

At the north end of the verandah the stair ascends to the upper storey. It requires little description: it was intended to have three shrines, as below; the south one, however, has not been commenced; the north one contains a squat, and the central a sitting Buddha with two attendants only. On the walls are many small Buddhas, a Padmapani with four arms, females with lotus-buds, etc.

* * *

Cave XII—The Tin Thal

The court of this fine cave has been thoroughly cleaned of the silt that filled it, and thus, thanks to the Nizam's Government, its ample area and great depth is now shown off to advantage. The labour in originally excavating such a court alone out of the solid rock must have been enormous.

Like the last, it is of three stories, the first entered by a few steps ascending from the court. It has eight square columns with bases, and plain brackets in the front, the upper portion of the central pair being covered with very pretty florid ornamentation. Behind the front row are other two of eight pillars each, and in the area that recedes back in the centre are six more columns, making thirty in all.

In a large compartment on the back wall, to the left of the approach to the shrine, is a sculpture in nine squares: in the centre Buddha with *chauri*-bearers; to his right and left Padmapani and Vajrapani; and, above and below, the six figures found in the shrines of Cave XI with book, sword, flag, and buds and flowers. This sculpture is repeated over and over again in different parts of this cave. In the corresponding position on the south side has been a seated Buddha, now quite destroyed. In three cells in the north side are stone couches for the monks. In central recesses right and left of the vestibule to the shrine are has squatting on *sinhasanas*, the left attendants ıg different flowers in each case.

)n each side the shrine door is a fat seated guardian, flower-stalks, that on the south side having the book ›ver the bud.

The shrine contains an enormous squat Buddha, over et from the seat to the crown of the head. High up ıch side wall are five squat Buddhas, and below are r sitting figures ; to the left, 1st, Padmapani with his ; 2nd, a figure with something very like a *crozier ;* with a sword over a flower; and 4th, with fruit and a On the right, 1st Vajrapani, defaced ; 2nd, a figure a flower ; 3rd, with flower-stalk and book ; 4th, with -bud. On the inside of the front wall are—on the ı a squatting female with a belt over her breasts ; and ıe south, one with four arms. a bottle, and a flower.

From the south end of the front aisle the stair ascends, from the first landing a room is entered on the south of the court, with two pillars in front. On the back is a Buddha on a high throne with his usual attend- ; and on the west side is Padmapani seated between a and female—the latter, perhaps, his wife.* There nany smaller figures, four-armed Devis, etc., in this ı.

From this the stair leads up to the first door. It has a open verandah in front, and a large central entrance ed by two square pillars leads into the hall. There ılso entrances from near each end of the verandah. e lead into a long hall 11 feet 5 inches high, divided three aisles by two rows of eight pillars each. On ends of the central vestibule are many sculptures,—

Those who seek for symbolism may perhaps interpret this as auddha triad or mystic ओम्. The lotus is the Bauddha emblem ative power ; and अ—the *Vija mantra* of the male Buddha, the ative power ; उ—the *Vija mantra* of the female Dharma (reli- law) or Adi Prajni, the type of productive power ; and म the *mantra* of the Sanga (assembly), the union of the essences of both.

among them Padmapani seated between two females, one of them with a bottle— a *dahgoba*, figures of Buddha, females, etc.

The shrine door has two fine *dvarapalas*. Padmapani on the north side holds a fully blown lotus and a rosary or *mala*, and the other his *vajra ;* both have jewelled belts, etc. Inside is an enormous squatting Buddha, and in front of the low throne is a female holding up a *lota*, and opposite her a smaller one standing over a prostrate figure. At the ends of the throne are large figures of Padmapani and Vajrapani with his emblem, and on each side wall four figures—with sword, flag, flower-buds, etc., while on the front wall are the usual male and female figures, which I have supposed to represent the patron of the cave and his wife. Above are seven squatting Buddhas on shelves.

In the north end of the verandah is Buddha sitting with the wheel behind his heels and two deer on the ground in front. On each side are his usual attendants and a standing Buddha—coarsely executed. From this the stair ascends, and in the jamb of the window at the first landing is a figure on horseback with two attendants ; above is a female with a flower.

The upper floor is the most striking among the Bauddha caves. It is divided into five cross aisles by rows of eight pillars, which with two in front of the shrine are forty-two in all, perfectly plain square columns moderately lofty. In recesses at the ends of the aisles are large figures of Buddhas seated on thrones, with their usual attendants. At the south end of the back aisle the Buddha is on a *sinhasana* with the wheel in the middle, and lying in front two finely cut deer, unfortunately broken by some barbarian. Possibly this may be intended as an allusion to Buddha's teaching in the *Mrigadava* or deer-park at Banaras—which seems to have been a favourite resort of his. In the north end of the same aisle Buddha is represented in a squatting attitude, his feet drawn up in front of him, and holding the little finger of his left hand with the thumb and forefinger of his right, as in the act of teaching. He sits on a lion-throne with a lion in the centre, but, instead of his usual attendants, on either side of him are (1) a squatting Buddha with hands in his lap in the act of ascetic meditation, by which he attained Buddhahood; (2) above this Buddha soaring to the heavens to preach his law to the Gods; and (3) Buddha dying or entering *Nirvana* —everlasting, undisturbed, unconscious repose. These are the great scenes in his life as a Teacher.

To the right of this figure, on a raised basement along the back wall as far as the vestibule to the shrine are seven squat meditative Buddhas all perfectly alike, except that each has the foliage of a different Bo-tree represented over his head springing from behind the nimbus or aureole. These are seven human or earth-born Buddhas, painted also in Cave XXII at Ajanta with the name below each, as Vipasya, Sikhi, Visvabhu, Krakutchanda, Kanaka Muni, Kasyapa, and Sakya Sinha. The Buddhists believe that the world is destroyed and regenerated at the end of immensely long periods or *kalpas*, and that each *kalpa* has one or more Buddhas to enlighten it: thus in the second *kalpa* before the present Vipasya was the Buddha; in the last Sikhi and Visvabhu; and in the present Krakutchanda, Kanaka Muni, Kasyapa, and Sakya Sinha; the religion established by the last being to prevail for 5,000 years after which Arya Maitreya, the Buddha of the future, is to appear and restore it.

On the south side of the vestibule is a similar row of seven meditating Buddhas, being perhaps the representations of the same personages, only with umbrellas as symbols of dominion, over their heads, instead of the Bo-trees. The Dhyani or divine Buddhas are only five:—(1) Vairochana, (2) Akshobhya, (3) Ratna Sambhava, (4) Amitabha, (5) Amogha Siddha—the mental creations of Adi Buddha, and each of whom respectively produced a Bodhisatva, *viz.* (1) Samanta Bhadra, (2) Vajrapani, (3) Ratnapani, (4) Padmapani, and (5) Visvapani. Had there been *seven* Dyhani Buddhas we might have supposed that this second group represented them.

The vestibule of the shrine contains two tall *dvarapalas* with crossed arms and lofty head-dresses ; on each end wall three female figures seated on a high basement, with the right foot down and resting on a lotus, and the left turned under her. The one next the corner on each side has ; four arms, and holds a *mala* or rosary and crooked rod ; she is doubtless some Hindu Devi, like Lakshmi or Sarasvati, introduced into the Bauddha mythology. On the back wall on each side are three similar figures, but all with two arms, and each holding some symbol as a flower, *vajra*, etc. They sit on *padmasanas*, or lotus-thrones, supported by Naga-canopied figures, standing among lotus-leaves, fish, birds, etc. They are, perhaps, female counterparts of the Bodhisatvas we have already met with in the shrine. Above all are four Buddhas on each division of the back wall, and five on each end wall.

In the shrine is the usual very large squat Buddha, which the natives persist in worshipping as Rama. His nose and lips have long been wanting, but these as well as mustachios are supplied in plaster, and whenever they fall or are knocked off their place is speedily supplied by fresh ones. On his left is (1) Padmapani, otherwise known as Avalokitesvara, with a *chauri* and, as usual, a small figure of Amitabha Buddha on the front of his cap : next to him is (2) a figure with a bud, then (3) one with a long sword in his right, and a flower in his left hand, (4) with a fruit and flower or small *chauri*, and (5) with some unrecognizable object and a branch or flower. On Buddha's left are (1) Vajrapani with his emblem above a flower-stalk which he holds, richly jewelled, and having a ring on his little finger ; (2) a figure with perhaps a book and fruit ; (3) with flower-buds ; (4) with a flag and a bud ; and (5) with a flower-stalk in the left hand, and perhaps a bag in the right hand. On the front wall a squatting female with a flower occupies the compartment to the north of the entrance, and on the south a fat male with a purse on his left knee, and perhaps money in his right hand. Below him is a *kamandala*, or jar with flowers growing out of it. Above on either side of the room are five squatting Buddhas, and on the front wall two more on each side—the same ten as on the back wall of the hall.

In the north side of the court of this cave is a small cave with two pillars in the east face, and which is reached by a stair from below. It is a square room and has a cistern in the floor.

* * *

Cave XIII

About forty yards to the north of the Tin Thal, the Brahmanical caves begin, the first being a large perfectly plain room. The front has been destroyed by the decay of the rock, and the floor is still deep in earth. It may have been a sort of *dharmasala*, or rest-house for visitors.

Cave XIV—Ravana-ka-Kai

Close to the last, which doubtless belonged to it, is an early Brahmanical cave, with four pillars in front and twelve inside the open hall, which measures 54 feet wide by 55½ to the front of the shrine. The shrine is surrounded by a wide passage or *pradakshina* for circumambulation, making the total depth of the excavation 85 feet. The central area is 14¼ feet high, and the side aisles 13 feet 8 inches.

Two pillars in front and one in the front aisle are gone. They have high square bases and drooping-eared florid capitals, with circular necks of varied patterns. The pilasters are carved from the floor to the brackets, and the compartments of the wall between them are filled with sculpture, but even within the last ten years the faces have been hacked and destroyed.

The south wall is covered with Saiva sculptures : beginning at the front they are—

1. Mahishasuri or Durga killing the buffalo-demon.

2. Siva and Parvati on a raised platform playing at *chausar* or *chaupta*, a sort of chess played with dice. Ganapati and another attendant wait behind Siva, and two females and a male behind Parvati, while between, but beyond them, Bhringi looks on at the game. Five of the faces in this compartment have been hacked within the last ten years. Below is Nandi, the bull of Siva, and thirteen small fat *ganas* rollicking.

3. Siva dancing the *tandava*, or great dance which he performs over the destruction of the world ; three figures with drums and fifes are to his right ; Bhringi, his skeleton attendant, is behind, and Parvati and two *ganas*—one with a cat's face—are on his left : above are Brahma and Vishnu on his left, and on his right Indra on his elephant, Agni on his ram, and two others.

4. Ravana, the demon king of Lanka or Ceylon, proud of his immeasurable strength, got under Kailasa, the white mountain or heaven of Siva, intending to carry it off; Parvati, got alarmed on feeling the place shake, and clung to Siva who fixed Ravana under the hill with his foot until he repented of his temerity. Ravana had ten heads and twenty arms, and often on the top of his cap an animal's head is represented, some say that of an ass. Four *ganas* here mock him. Siva and Parvati have each their attendants, and two guardians stand at the sides.

5. Bhairava, the destructive form of Siva, his foot on a large fat dwarf, another at his side, Ganapati behind him, holding up with two of his hands the elephant-hide in which he wraps himself ; with other two he holds the spear with which he has transfixed Ratnasura ; in one is a long sword, and in a sixth a bowl to receive the blood of his victim.

These last four are frequently represented in other caves with more or less detail.

6. In the *pradakshina* on this side is a remarkable group. The first portion of it is very much in shade, but consists of three skeletons ; Kal, four-armed with a scorpion on his breast, Kali, the female personification of

Death ; and a third kneeling. Then comes Ganapati eating his favourite *ladus*, beyond whom are the seven divine mothers, four-armed, each with a child, and, on the base below, her cognizance—(1) perhaps Chamunda with the owl, (2) Indrani with the elephant, (3) Varahi with the boar, (4) Vaishnavi or Lakshmi with Garuda, (5) Kaumari with the peacock, (6) Maheshvari with the bull and (7) Brahmi, Brahmani or Sarasvati with the *hansa* or goose.* On the return of the wall at the back is Siva seated with the mace or axe and *damru* or small hand-drum.

On the north wall, commencing from the front, are—

1. Bhavani or Durga, four-armed, with her foot resting on her tiger, holding a *trisula* or trident in her upper right hand ; the others are broken.

2. Lakshmi the wife of Vishnu, over a mass of lotuses, with Naga-canopied figures holding up water-jars, and a tortoise among them. She has two arms, but her attendants on each side holding water-pots have four ; one on her right also holds a *sankha* or conch, one of the symbols of Vishnu. Elephants bathe her with water from jars.

3. Varaha, the boar-incarnation of Vishnu, his foot on Sesha the great serpent, holding up Prithvi, the personification of the Earth, whom he rescues from destruction. A snake-demon is between his feet, and figures with Naga-hoods, over their heads stand on each side, one supplicating.

4. Vishnu, four-armed, in his heaven of Vaikuntha, sitting between his wives Lakshmi and Sita, and four attendants behind with *chauris*. Below is Garuda, the man-eagle on which Vishnu travels, and several males and females, some of them playing on musical instruments.

5. Vishnu and Lakshmi seated on the same couch under a *torana* or ornamental arch, with attendants behind. Below are seven dwarfs seated, four of them with musical instruments.

* See *Indian Antiquary*, Vol. VI. p. 74, note ||

The front of the shrine has two very tall male *dvara-palas* and a number of other figures, principally females and attendant dwarfs, fat *gandharvas* with curly wigs and garlands, etc. Inside is an altar against the back wall, and a broken image of Bhavani or Durga, to whom this cave-temple was doubtless dedicated. There are four holes, as if for fire-pits (*agni-kundas*) in the floor of the hall.

Cave XV—The Das Avatara

To the next cave there is a very considerable ascent up the rock by means of steps. Like the last two Buddhist caves, the whole court has been hewn out of the solid rock, leaving a curtain wall across the front of it, and a sacrificial hall in the middle, with a number of small shrines and a water-cistern in the surrounding walls. This hall has had a porch to the west, supported by two square pillars in front of a perforated window, over which is a long Sanskrit inscription too much obliterated for translation. The entrance faces the cave on the east, and inside it has four pillars on a raised platform in the floor. In the back aisle is a single round fire-pit. The outer walls have a good deal of figure carving, and the flat roof is surmounted outside by lions at the corners, and fat human figures between along the edges.

The cave is of two stories, the lower being a few feet above the level of the court, and supported by fourteen plain square pillars and measuring 95 feet in length, with two cells in the back wall near each end. In the north end of the front aisle the stair ascends, and is lighted by a window at the landing, where it turns to the right. On the wall of this landing are eleven compartments, each about two feet high, with bas-reliefs. They are (1) Ganapati in the window-jamb; (2) Parvati on Siva's knee; (3) Surya or Vishnu with a lotus in each hand, and two attendants; (4) Siva and Parvati with small figures of Ganapati, Nandi, and Vishnu on Garuda below; (5) Mahishasuri, the head of the buffalo struck off, and the Asura coming out of the neck; (6) Ardhanari or half-male half-female form

KAILASA : MAIN SHRINE AND DHWAJASTHAMBHA

of Siva, four-armed, with *trisula* and looking-glass; (7) Bhavani, four-armed, on her tiger, with *trisula* and *damru*; (8) Ganapati; (9) Uma or Parvati with water-pot and rosary, practising *tapas* or asceticism between two fires, with Brahma and others looking on; (10) Ardhanari; and (11) Kali or Bhavani four-armed, with sword, *trisula*, bowl, and a piece of flesh at which a dog snatches.

Another flight of steps leads into the end of the front aisle of the great hall above, 95 feet wide by 109 deep inclusive of the vestibule to the shrine, supported by forty-four square columns, including two in front of the vestibule of the shrine. Those in front are richly carved with floral ornamentations, in which dwarfs, snakes, etc., are also introduced. Like the last cave, the sculptures on one side are mostly Vaishnava, and on the other entirely Saiva. Outside the front at either end is a gigantic Saiva *dvarapala*. Between the pilasters in each end are deep recesses filled with large sculptures, mostly in almost entire relief; and some of them cut with great boldness and power. Beginning on the north side, with the Saiva sculptures—the first from the door is Bhairava or Mahadeva in his terrible form; and a more vivid picture of the terrible a very diseased imagination only could embody. The gigantic figure lounges forward holding up his elephant-hide, with necklace of skulls (*mundmala*) depending below his loins; round him a cobra is knotted; his open mouth showing his large teeth, while with his *trisula* he has transfixed one victim, who, writhing on its prongs, seems to supplicate pity from the pitiless; while he holds another by the heels with one of his left hands, raising the *damru* as if to rattle it in joy while he catches the blood with which to quench his demon-thirst. To add to the elements of horror, Kali, gaunt and grim, stretches her skeleton length below, with huge mouth, bushy hair, and sunken eyeballs, having a crooked knife in her right hand, and stretching out the other with a bowl, as if eager to share in the gore of the victim; behind her head is the owl or vampire, as fit witness of the scene. On the right, in front of the skeleton, is Parvati; and higher up, near the foot of the victim Ratnasura, is a grinning face drawing out its tongue. Altogether the group is a picture of the devilish. The very armlets Bhairava wears are ogre faces.

The second chapel contains Siva dancing the *tandava*; the third contains an altar, perhaps for Bhavani, never quite finished; the fourth is Siva and Parvati at the game of *chausar*, with Nandi and the rollicksome *ganas* below; the fifth contains the marriage scene of Siva and Parvati, in which, contrary to the usual representations, she is at his left side. Brahma with triple face squats below to perform the priestly functions, while above are the Gods, riding on various animals, as witnesses of the scene. The sixth chapel contains the usual representation of Ravana under Kailasa.

On the back wall we have first Siva springing out of the *linga* to protect his worshipper Markandeya, whom Yama, the Hindu Pluto, has noosed and is about to drag off to his dark abode. The second has Siva and Parvati. Siva holds a lock of his hair with one hand, and a *mala* in the other. On his right is the bull Nandi, and beyond it is Bhringi; over him is an elephant, and above this a squatting ascetic. To the left of the nimbus round Siva's head is a deer.

We now come to the ante-chamber or vestibule of the shrine. On the left end of it is a huge Ganapati. On the floor at the back corners are lions, carved with considerable spirit. On the back wall, left of the shrine door, is Parvati with a rosary, and on each side of her, musicians. She sits on a *padmasana* upheld by two figures among the leaves. The *dvarapalas* of the shrine are four-armed, with snake, club, and *vajra*. Inside the sanctuary the *salunkha* or altar, round the *linga* or emblem of Siva, is broken.

To the right of the shrine door is Lakshmi or Sri, with four elephants pouring water upon her while two male attendants offer jars of water and hold the *sankha*, *chakra* or discus, and lotus : she has a lotus and a *sitaphal* or custard-apple. In the south end of this vestibule is Vishnu with his lotus and *trisula,* somewhat differing from Siva's, with a large bird (Garuda ?) at his right hand.

In the south side of the back wall is, 1st, Siva inside a *linga* with flames issuing from the sides of it. Vishnu is represented below on the right as Varaha–the boar-*avatara* —digging down to see if he can reach the base of the great *linga ;* having failed to do so, he is also represented as worshipping it. On the other side is Brahma ascending to discover the top of it, which he also failed to do, and stands as a worshipper. Thus Siva is said to have proved to these rival divinities his own superiority to both of them. 2nd, Siva, having seized the chariot of the sun, made the four *Vedas* his horses, and Brahma his charioteer, going out to war against the Asura Taraka.

We now come to the south wall, and proceeding towards the front we have, 1st, Vishnu, six-armed, his left foot on a dwarf holding up the hill Govardhan to protect the flocks of Vraj from the deluge of rain Indra sent down. 2nd, Vishnu Narayana resting on Sesha, the great serpent, with a human head and five hoods ; while out of Vishnu's navel springs a lotus on which Brahma is seated. Lakshmi rubs her lords's feet, and seven figures are represented below. 3rd, Vishnu riding on Garuda. 4th, a *salunkha* or altar, which has been protected by a high screen in front. 5th, Varaha, the boar-*avatara* of Vishnu, holding Prithvi (the Earth) on his hand, with three snake-figures or Nagas below. 6th, Vishnu in the Vamana or dwarf incarnation in which he deceived the good king Bali, obtaining from him a promise of all he could cover at three strides. The dwarf then burst into tremendous proportions, strode over earth and heaven at two strides, and, though Bali tried to appease him with a pot full of precious stones, nothing would do but a third stride, and placing his foot on Bali he thrust him down to Patala, or Hell. Garuda behind him binds a prisoner. (There is a doubt about the interpretation of this scene.) 7th,

Nrisinha, or the lion-*avatara* of Vishnu, wrestling with his enemy, who is armed with sword and shield, but with two arms can have no fair chance with his eight-armed enemy. Outside the front pillars is a gigantic Saiva *dvarapala* at each side.

Cave XVI—Kailasa, or the Rang Mahal

Kailasa is one of the most remarkable of all the cave-temples in India, and were there no others at Elura, such as the Visvakarma, Tin Thal, Dumar Lena, and Indra Sabha it would alone be worth a long journey to see. Indeed, were it not for the other large cave-temples beside it, Kailasa would probably be thought more highly of; but the visitor, in order to see the others, hurries over Kailasa too hastily to take in its size, the profusion of its sculptures, and the vast labour that it must have demanded to execute it.

All the sculptures and the whole architectural style of the central temple impress me with the conviction that it is later than the Papanath temple at Pattadkal, but probably earlier than the great Saiva temple of Virupakshadeva there*. It has at one time all been painted in a style befitting its elaborateness of sculpture. This painting has been renewed again and again, perhaps in a continuous succession of debased styles, the latest certainly poor enough. But there are still some bits in the roof of the porch, of two or three successive coatings, that would compare favourably even among many of the Ajanta paintings.

The lofty basement of the temple is of itself a remarkable conception, with its row of huge elephants and *sardulas* or lions, griffins, etc., in every possible attitude, tearing one another or feeding. And then the great hall above, with its sixteen pillars and more pilasters, all carved with different details of sculpture; its balcony porches at the sides, and double pavillions before the front porch; its vestibule to the sanctuary, with large sculptures on each

* See my *First Archæological Report for Western India.*

side; and its five shrines round the outside of the principal one and on the same platform, all testify to the attempt made to rival and outdo all previous temples of the kind.

Dedicated to Siva, it is surrounded with figures also of Vishnu and the whole Puranic pantheon. Its sculptures bear testimony to the prevalence of the eclectic Smartta school, and the degradation of morals which led, in the south of India, to the rise of the Lingavats, and made it necessary that external influence should be brought to bear on a people drunk with idolatry and enervated by the lusts it encouraged, in order to save them from utter destruction. With all his wealth of imaginative device, the Hindu artist could not help betraying the depravity of his nature, any more than those of other nations unenlightened by Christianity. The sword of Islam, if it did not stop the worship of idols, reminded the people and their chiefs of other employments than the debauchery of temple festivals and dances, and the repetition of inane *mantras;* and a ruthless soldiery revealed to them the inability of their Gods to save, or their effeminate worshippers to contend with truly brave though cruel men. Now the Indian Muhammadan worships the tombs of the dead with more bigoted idolatry than the Hindu; and his Faqirs are quite as filthy and ignorant as the Saiva Jogis.

The interior, and parts at least if not the whole, of the exterior, have been plastered over and painted, and where this has not very long ago peeled off has had the effect of preserving the stone inside from the smoke of wandering *jogis'* and travellers' fires, with which it must for ages have been saturated.

Unlike any of the preceding cave-temples, Kailasa is a great monolithic temple isolated from surrounding rock, and carved outside as well as in. It stands in a great court averaging 154 feet wide by 276 long at the level of the base, entirely cut out of the solid rock, and with a scarp 107 feet high at the back. In front of this court a curtain has been left, carved on the outside with the monstrous forms of Siva and Vishnu and their congeners, and with rooms inside it. It is pierced in the centre by an entrance passage with rooms on each side. Passing this the visitor is met by a large sculpture of Lakshmi over the lotuses, with her attendant elephants. There are some letters and a date on the leaves of the lotus on which she sits, but illegible, and probably belonging to the 15th century. On the bases of the pilasters on each side have been inscriptions in characters of the 8th century, but of that on the left side only two letters remain, while on the other may be read doubtfully—

Bhu..rasya
si halakirnna
........*dhachna*

Here we enter, to right and left, the front portion of the court which is a few feet lower than the rest, and at the north and south ends of which stand two gigantic elephants,—that on the south much mutilated. Turning again to the east and ascending a few steps, we enter the great court occupied by the temple, whose base measures 164 feet from east to west by 109 where widest from north to south. In front of it and connected by a bridge is a *mandapa* for the Nandi, and on each side this *mandapa* stands a pillar or *dhvajadanda*—'ensign staff'—45 feet high, or with what remains of the *trisula* of Siva on top—making the total height about 49 feet.

Under the bridge connecting the temple with the *mandapa* are two large sculptures,—on the west Siva as Kal Bhairava with flaming eyes and in a state of frenzied excitement, with the *Saptamatra* at his feet; on the other he is represented almost exactly in th ascetic attitude of Buddha—as Mahayogi the great ascetic, with attendant *munis,* hermits, and Gods. At each side of this bridge a stair leads up to the great hall of the temple. On the outer wall of the south stair is carved, in a series of lines, the story of the *Ramayana* or war of Rama, aided by Hanuman and his monkeys with Ravana the demon-king of Lanka ; and on the north side some of the episodes from the other Hindu epic—the *Mahabharata* or account of the great war between the Pandavas aided by Krishna, and their relatives the Kauravas. Behind these sculptures the lofty basement of the temple commences, with its row of huge elephants, etc.,—feeding, tearing one another, or trampling the bowels out of others, etc., while apparently supporting the temple above. This line is unbroken except on the south side, where there has been a bridge across from a balcony of the temple to a cave in the scarp, but the bridge has long since fallen. Under this is a somewhat spirited sculpture of Ravana under Kailasa. Parvati is stretched out clinging to Siva ; while her maid, in fright at the shaking of the ground under her feet, is represented in the background fleeing for safety. To see this properly we ascend into an unfinished cave in the south side of the court. A door in the east end of it leads into the corridor which surrounds the whole back half of the court. On the south side it measures 118 feet in length. The back is divided by pilasters into twelve compartments, each containing a large sculpture. They are as follows :—

1. Perhaps Anna Purna, four-armed holding a water-pot, rosary, spike or bud, and wearing her hair in the *jata* style, resembling Lakshmi. 2. Said to be Siva as Balaji who slew Indrajit the son of Ravana, but very like Vishnu, four-armed, with club, discus or *chakra*, and *sankha* or conch, with a supplicant, and a small female figure in front of his club. 3. Vishnu, four-armed, with the *sankha*, holding by the tail the seven-hooded snake Kaliya, armed with a sword, with his foot on its breast. 4. Varaha raising Prithvi ; he is four-armed, with *chakra* and *sankha*, and has the snake under his foot. 5. A four-armed Vishnu on Garuda, the man-eagle that carries him. 6. The Vamana or dwarf incarnation of Vishnu, six-armed, with long sword, club, shield, *chakra*, and *sankha*, with his foot uplifted over the head of Bali holding his pot of jewels, as in the Das Avatara. 7. A four-armed Vishnu uphold-

ing the lintel of the compartment, intended to represent the base of a hill, over the flocks of Vraj. 8. Sesha Narayana, or Vishnu, on the great snake, and Brahma on the lotus springing from his navel, with five fat little figures below. 9. Nrisinha, or the lion-incarnation of Vishnu tearing out the entrails of his enemy. 10. A figure with three faces (Brahma) and four arms trying to pull up the *linga*. 11. Siva, four-armed, with his bull Nandi. 12. Ardhanari, or the combined male and female personification of Siva, four-armed, with Nandi.

This concludes the south corridor, and here we enter the east one, 189 feet in length, with nineteen compartments :—

1. Siva, locally known as Kal Bhairava, four-armed, with *trisula ;* and a small figure of Parvati, her hair done up in a peculiar style. 2. Siva (or Kapal Bhairava) stepping out from lotuses, with a small figure of Parvati holding him by the finger. 3. Siva (Nauyogini Bhairava) four-armed, with *trisula*, one right hand on Parvati's head, the other on her breast. 4. Siva (Siddhi Yogini Bhairava), four-armed, with *trisula* in his left hand, *gandharvas* above, and attendant below. 5. Siva (Baltuka Bhairava), four-armed, dancing on a dwarf with a long-shafted *trisula* in one of his left hands. 6. A Siva, (Bhupal Bhairava), with only a ribbon over his thighs, *trisula* over his right shoulder, bowl in left hand, and *damru* in right,—Parvati in front of him. 7. Siva or Bhairava, four-armed, as usual, with Nandi on his right and Parvati on his left, holding a cobra. 8. Siva or Mahadeva, four-armed, with Nandi. 9. Brahma with his *hansa* or sacred goose, three-faced and four armed, with ascetic's waterpot and rosary or *japa-mala*. 10. Siva with cobra and Nandi. 12. The same with *trisula*, Nandi, and a figure worshipping him. 13. Siva with snake holding a lock of his hair, while the Ganges perhaps is represented as flowing from his hair outside the arm ; a *gandharva* over his head ; Parvati at his left ; an elephant at his right ; above, a figure like Brahma. 14. Siva in

ing linga, with Brahma, Varaha, and Vishnu, as
Das Avatara. 15. Perhaps Siva with four arms,
damru club, and bell. 16. Siva and Parvati sitting
—Nandi below. 17. Sadasiva, six-armed, going
against Tripurasura; Brahma with six hands,
and Nandi borne as an ensign or *dhvaja*. 18.
dra, six-armed, with *damru*. *trisula*, and bowl to
e blood of Ratnasura— for every drop of it that
he ground produced another demon like himself
ding one of a well-known Greek fable; Kali,
the goblin Bhringi, and, an owl or vampire are
resented. 19. The marriage—Parvati on Siva's
e holds a flower and lays his hand in one of hers,
rahma is represented below.

ning now to the west into the north corridor, 120
g with twelve compartments, we have :—1. Siva
g the sage Markandeya against Yama. 2. Siva and
shippers,—perhaps the Kiratas,—one with a bow,
l snake. 3. Siva and Parvati playing at *chausar*;
and eleven *ganas* below. 4. Siva and Parvati
together; Narada below seems to be playing a
strument for their Godship's delectation. 5. Siva
vati with her arm entwined in his; Ravana was
d to be represented below, shaking Kailasa, but
pture was left unfinished. 6. A two-armed figure
Rishi Muchhkund) with a bag on his left shoulder.
and Parvati seated facing each other;—perhaps
lating some *Purana* or story to her. 8. Siva
ahmans say Kartikeya his son) with cobra and
and Nandi to his right. 9. Siva and Parvati
and Nandi couchant below. 10. The same pair
inga altar between them—for Parvati to worship;
elow. 11. Siva with Parvati on his left knee,
ed and a standing figure below. And 12. Below,
ing figure of Ravana upholding the *salunkha* or
which is a linga, with nine of his heads, which
lready cut off, around it, while he is in the act of
off the tenth; at this juncture Siva, pleased with

his devotion, interferes, and tells him to ask any boon he chooses when, as a proper demand to so rash a promise, he asks for Parvati, who is only recovered by a vile stratagem.

While passing along these corridors the visitor has the best opportunity of studying the variety in and effects of the great elephant base that surrounds the central temple.

A door from the last corridor leads into a continuation of it, 57 feet but without sculptures at the back: the two front pillars, however, as seen from the court, are elegantly ornamented.

Descending from this last portion of the corridor by the steps in front of it, we may now enter the north staircase leading up to the porch of the great shrine. On the roof of this porch are some bits of the ancient fresco paintings, of two or three successive coatings, that may help to give an idea of the style of decoration that at one time covered the whole of this great fane. The door is guarded by gigantic Saiva *dvarapalas*, leaning on heavy maces. The hall, 57 feet wide by 55 deep, has a wide central and cross aisle, while in each corner thus formed four massive square columns support the roof. The four round the central area are of one pattern, differing only in the details of their sculptures; the remaining twelve are also of one general type; while the sixteen pilasters are more of the style of the four central columns. At each end of the cross aisle is a door leading out into a side balcony, with two pillars in front of it richly carved in florid ornamentation.

At the east end of the hall is the vestibule of this shrine. On the roof is Lakshmi or Anna Purna, standing on a lotus, with high *jata* head-dress. Brahma squats at her right elbow, Vishnu (?) at her left with *gandharvas* at the corners of the sculpture. On the north wall of this vestibule *was* Siva and Parvati engaged at *chausar* now almost totally destroyed above; on the south was Siva and Parvati upon Nandi couching on a slab supported by four *ganas*, and a fifth at the end. Siva has a child on his right knee, and behind him are four attendants.

The *dvarapalas* were females,—probably Ganga and Yamuna, one on a *makara*, and the other on a tortoise, but the heads of both have been destroyed.

The shrine is a plain cell 15 feet square inside, with a large rosette on the roof. The present altar or *salunkha* is a modern affair. What originally occupied it is uncertain; it was probably a *linga*-shrine from the first, though the female *dvarapalas* might suggest that the Ranga Mahal, or Painted Palace, was dedicated to one of the forms of Parvati or Bhavani.

A door in each of the back corners of the hall leads to the terrace behind, on which a wide path leads quite round the outside of the shrine, which forms the base of the *vimana, sikhar* or spire. This spire rises to a height of 96 feet from the court below, and is all elaborately carved. Below are compartments between pilasters, with richly sculptured finials over each, and the centre of each compartment occupied in most cases by some form of Siva, with Vishnu, however, in some. On the wall above these are flying figures, and over them the horizontal mouldings of the *sikhar* begin.

On the outer side of this platform are five small shrines in four of which are altars as if for the worship of Goddesses; the fifth is empty.

Returning to the entrance of the hall we find, across the bridge, outside the porch, a small pavilion with four doors and a broken Nandi in it—probably not the original, for this is but a small bull; and beyond this to the west are a number of chambers over the entrance porch. From these there is access to the roof of the small chambers in front of the court, from which good views along each side of the great temple can be had.

Descending again to the court by the south staircase, we may scramble up (for the steps are broken away) into a cave about 37 feet by 15, with two square pillars and pilasters in front, each pillar having a tall female warder with her hair hanging towards her left shoulder in loose folds and with two dwarf attendants. Behind each pillar on the floor is a low square pedestal, as if for an altar; and round the three inner sides of this *yajnashala*, or sacrificial hall, as it is sometimes called, are the female monsters the Brahmans delighted to teach their votaries to revere as the mothers of creation. First on the west end comes, Vaghesvari four-armed, with *trisula*, and under her feet the tiger; then a second, somewhat similar figure; and next, Kal, a grinning skeleton with cobra girdle and necklace, seated on two dying men—a wolf gnawing the leg of one,—while behind him is Kali, and another skeleton companion. On the back wall is (1) Ganapati as usual. (2) A female, almost quite destroyed, with a child, sitting on a wolf. (3) Indrani also destroyed. (4) Parvati (?), with a bull in front of the seat as a cognizance, her head and the child destroyed. (5) Vaishnavi, her arms and the child destroyed, Garuda below. (6) Karttikeyi, bust gone child crawling on the knee, with peacock holding a snake as *chinha* or cognizance. (7) A Devi with *trisula*, and having a humped bull below. (8) Sarasvati holding a rosary. (9) Another Devi, two of her four arms broken off, holding a shallow vessel. On the east end are three female seated figures without the nimbus and cognizance that mark the others, and each holding a *chauri* or fly-flap: these are separated from the preceding by a fat dwarf who sits with his back to these three. All these figures are quite separate from the wall, and form a somewhat imposing assemblage.

Descending to the court again: under the west end of the *yajnashala* is a small low cave, the verandah divided from the inner room by a *torana* or arch from two attached pillars. Inside is an altar for some idol, probably a moveable one.

Opposite the sculpture of Ravana already described, the ascent to a cave above may be effected by means of a ladder. The verandah is 61 feet by 22, inclusive of the two pillars in front, and inside is a dark hall with four heavy plain pillars, 55 feet by 34,—the shrine scarcely more than begun. A stair at the west end of the verandah leads to a third storey, with similar verandah and hall, but lighted by two windows, besides the door and by an opening in the roof up into a small cave that may be noticed at the road-side on the ascent of the ghat; its four pillars support arches on the four sides of the central square.

Passing now to the north side of the court: nearly opposite the obelisk we enter a corridor 60 feet long, with five pillars in the front. At the east end is an ascent of two or three steps to a figure of Sri or Lakshmi, Goddess of prosperity, with a lotus in each hand, and four attendant elephants. The stair to the left of this is badly lighted, but ascends to a fine cave called Lanka or Lankesvara, 123 feet long from the back of the Nandi to the back of the *pradakshina*, and 60 wide inside the front screen. The roof is low, and supported by 27 massive pillars, besides pilasters, some of them very richly carved, but evidently of a later style than the central temple. On entering from the stair a low screen-wall, connecting the west line of pillars, faces the visitor; to the left, and directly in front of the Nandi, which occupies a large recess in this end, is the entrance into the hall.

On the inner side of each of the pillars on the south face, which are also connected by a low screen, is a sculpture. They have been cut with considerable care, and the stone being in this place very close-grained the carving has been sharp, and would have stood for ages had not the bigotry of ignorant iconoclasts spared no pains to deface the inoffensive stone,—flattering themselves that by so gratifying their own low passions they were doing something to purchase divine favour. In the south-west corner was Mahishasuri; on the second pillar Ardhanari,—the face and breast broken, perhaps not very long since; the third was Bhairava or Virabhadra, terribly mutilated; the fourth Siva and Parvati—entirely gone except the feet; and the fifth, Siva with his left foot on a dwarf, and

Parvati at his right hand. At the end of the aisle has been boldly executed Siva dancing the *tandava*, with a skull withering in his head-dress.

On the right-hand side of the entrance to the *pradakshina* is a sculpture of Siva and Parvati with Ravana below, and maid running off; in the north entrance are the same Gods playing at *chausar*, the board distinctly represented, a plantain-tree behind, and the Nandi and *ganas* below.

On each side the shrine door is a female guardian, one standing on a *makara*, the other on a *kurma* or tortoise,—probably Ganga and Yamuna. The *salunkha* or altar inside the shrine has been smashed. On the back wall of the shrine, in very low relief, is a grotesque *Trimurti*, or bust of Siva with three faces, representative of three phases of his supposed character as Creator (Brahma), Preserver (Vishnu), and Destroyer (Rudra).

In the back aisle of the cave are a series of pretty large sculptures:—1. At the east end is Vishnu, perhaps as Surya, with two hands, holding flowers, and with a male and female on each side holding buds,—one with a spear and oval shield. 2. On the back wall, Varaha holding up Prithivi. 3. Parvati or Uma between two fires, four-armed, and holding up Ganapati as a *dhvaja* or ensign. 4. In the middle compartment are three figures,—in the centre Siva, four-armed, with *trisula* and cobra, Nandi on his left, and an attendant on right; to the left of Siva is Vishnu; and to the right a three-faced Brahma. 5. In the next recess is Nrisinha, the lion-*avatara* of Vishnu, tearing the bowels out of his victim, and supported by Garuda and *ganas*. 6. A large Ganapati.

On each side the recess for Nandi is a four-armed *dvarapala*, with huge clubs and axe-edges protruding from the heads of them.

In a small cave at the east end of the front of Lankesvara are the *Saptamatra* on a small scale, and some remains of grotesque paintings.

Descending from this to the court, just behind the elephant, is a small shrine with two pillars in front, and the back divided into three compartments. In the first (to the right) a tall female stands on a tortoise, with creepers and water-plants behind her: the feet have been very carefully carved, but the guard have used the floor for mixing lime on, and the legs are broken. In the second is a similar figure on a *makara*, with lotus leaves and flowers behind her. In the third she stands on a lotus; in the back ground are creepers with birds among their leaves and branches. These figures must be Ganga, Yamuna, and Sarasvati.

It would only weary the reader to describe all the multitudinous sculptures that cover the walls of this great fane.

Small Caves

On the north side of Kailasa by a footpath leading up to the plateau, we reach some small caves, in the shrine of one of the first of which is a *Trimurti*. A good way higher up, and not easily discovered, are some larger ones. About a quarter of a mile further north, on the sides of the stream that comes over the cliff close to the last Brahmanical cave, is a considerable group of cells and small shrines. Some of these are curious from their having small open courts entered by a door with Dravidian pediment upon it, others have *Trimurtis* on the back wall of the shrines, which have round *salunkhas* and *lingas* in them. On the ceiling of two of them are some pieces of painting still left.

* * *

Cave XVII

The next large cave north of Kailasa is across a deep ravine, and till 1876 was filled to a depth of 6 or 7 feet with earth, so that only the capitals of the pillars were visible. It was, however, well worth excavating, and has been cleaned with care, and without damage to the carving. This and the next are called by the natives "Dumar Lena,"—a name, however, which has been attached by Europeans to Cave XXIX.

This is a Saiva temple with three rows of four pillars from side to side: the front and back aisles being 64 feet long, and the depth up to the front of the shrine 37 feet, or over all 76 feet. In front has been a porch raised by seven or eight steps above the level of the court, on two massive square pillars, one of which is gone, and the other reduced to a shapeless mass principally by the weather and a *pipal* tree. Surrounding the court on three sides has been a low covered corridor with a small door in the centre of the front for ingress. Over this corridor, at each end of the facade is a sculptured compartment: that on the south contains Brahma with two female attendants and two *gandharvas* on clouds: the other probably Vishnu, four-armed with female attendants;—a hole broken through the lower portion of it opens into the verandah of the next cave.

The extreme pillars of the front are plain square ones with bracket capitals; the inner pair have deep brackets on two sides, carved with female figures and dwarf attendants. The middle pair in the next row have cushion capitals with female figures, etc. as struts on their inner sides, and fat dwarfs on the corners of the high square bases; the brackets above have not been finished. The outer pillars in this and the next row are in section "broken squares," so favourite a form in later structural temples,—the form being that of a square with thin pilasters of less breadth attached to each side. The middle pillars in the next row are unlike any others here: the base is of the "broken square" pattern, with female figures carved on the principal faces, and males on the corner ones. Over this is a Dravidian moulding as in the pilasters of Ravana-ka-Kai, then a belt with floral ornament in the centre, and two dwarfs at each corner. Over this is a 16-sided neck, and then the struts with female figures and attendants on three sides. These columns are too heavy to be elegant.

The shrine door is boldly moulded in Dravidian style. The *dvarapalas* have each only two hands, and hold flowers —no clubs, but each is attended by his dwarf and *gandharvas*. Inside is a large square *salunkha* and decayed *linga*. The *pradakshina* is entered by a door on each side the shrine.

The only sculptures on the walls inside are,—Mahishasuri on the south end of the front aisle, and Ganapati—four-armed—on the north, both well preserved, from having been so long buried in the earth.

Cave XVIII

This is close to the last, and measures 67 feet by 55 over all. It has four clumsy unfinished columns in front, and a deep recess at each end inside. At the back of the hall is a vestibule or ante-chamber to the shrine 30 feet by 10½, with two pillars and corresponding pilasters in front. Some plaster, consisting of mud with vegetable fibres in it, adheres to parts of the walls and pillars of this cave, and on one of the last a few letters of a painted inscription in Devanagari are still visible. In the shrine is a round *salunkha* set on a base, and of a different stone from the cave.

In front, in the usual place for the Nandi, is a square trough : possibly an *agnikunda* or fire-pit.

Cave XIX

Descending to a slightly lower level, a little further along the scarp, we come to a primitive-looking cave. Part of the roof has fallen in ; it has not been excavated ; the rain water stands long in it, and it stinks from the bats that infest it. The front pillars have gone, and for some distance inside the entrance the cave is not so wide as it is in the middle, where four pillars on each side screen off recesses ; in line with the fourth of these are four more in front of the shrine, which contains a broken *salunkha* and *linga*. The pillars are very rude attempts at the Elephanta style with cushion-shaped capitals.

Close to the next is another unexcavated cave, all ruined, and hidden by underwood.

Cave XX

Ascending again, we come to a small *linga* shrine, originally with two pillars in front,—now gone, but which, as the pilasters show, were probably of the Elephanta pattern. Outside the facade on the north is Ganapati, and on the south Mahishasuri. The shrine has a wide *pradakshina* round it, and in each entrance to it is a large cell with two square pillars, having octagon necks in front. Inclusive of these chambers this cave measures 53 feet by 30 over all.

The shrine door is carved round with *veli* or creeper and roll patterns. On each side is a tall *dvarapala*, with a smaller female figure between him and the entrance.

Cave XXI.—Ramesvara

Close to the last, and behind a fine large platform, is a lofty and interesting Saiva temple, locally known as Ramesvara. In the court before it, on a lofty pedestal with *bas-reliefs* on the sides of it, couches the Nandi; in a chapel on the north side with two pillars in front is Ganapati, and between it and the pilaster is a gigantic female standing on a *makara*, with dwarf attendants, *chauri*-bearer, and *gandharvas*. On the south side is a similar figure on a tortoise. A screen wall half the height of the pillars connects the front ones. The capitals of the four in front are carved in representation of a water-vessel (*kamandala*) with plants growing out of it and drooping over on each side. To this are added struts carved with female figures standing under foliage, with their attendant dwarfs. On the brackets above are horned monster *grasdas*. The frieze above is carved in compartments of arabesques divided by fat *ganas*.

RAMESHWAR : FACADE WITH FIGURE BRACKETS

The hall is 15½ feet high and measures 69 feet by 251 with a chapel at each end, cut off by two cushion-capital pillars. Each of these chapels is surrounded by sculptures. In the south one we find—1. On the right wall, a tall four-armed ghastly skeleton with a broad, short, pointed knife; another skeleton clasps his leg while it looks up to *Kali*, just behind, who seizes it by the hair, while she holds a dissevered head in her left hand, and wears a snake (not a cobra) round her neck. Another skeleton, also with a snake round its neck, grins over her head. A more hideous group could not well be conceived. In front of the tall skeleton (*Kal*) stands a figure with a sword, and overhead is a *gandharva* with an offering. 2. On the back wall is Ganesa, seven four-armed Devis (the *Saptamatra*), and a musician. The *chinhas* below are mostly rotted away. Except in the elaborateness of their head-dresses they are nearly the same as already described. 3. On the east end is Siva dancing, eight-armed, while Gods riding on peacock, elephant, ox, Garuda, etc. appear in the clouds over his shoulders; Parvati and attendants, with four musicians, look on below, and a small Bhringi dances behind Siva's leg.

In the north chapel are,—1. On the left end, a tall four-armed figure standing with a chick in one left hand, and holding a large bird by the neck with the other; right and left are attendants with rams' heads. On the back wall are—2. Brahma seated on a chair, with an attendant behind him, addressing a squatting figure with a female behind. 3. The marriage of Siva—Brahma on the extreme left, with a fire before him, while a bearded figure is seated on the other side of it. Behind him are two males, one carrying a box. Then comes Parvati or Uma, with a female behind her, and a male with a round jar: Siva takes Parvati's hand, and in front is a small figure of Ganesa, while behind Siva is a dwarf and four other attendants—one with a *sankha*. 4. Parvati or Uma, the daughter of Himalaya, as an ascetic, amidst four fires, a rosary in one hand, and rocks behind her: this *tapas* she undertook to gain the love of Siva. Her maid kneels at her right hand, and on her left is a tall female with a box. Siva or a Yogi approaches her with a water-bottle, and behind him are lotuses, and overhead fruits. Next, to the right, is a tall female addressing a figure,—possibly Kamadeva or Makaradhvaj, the Hindu Cupid,–with shaven crown, coming out of a *makara's* mouth ; and behind him is another male figure. 5. On the base of this tableau is a most remarkable row of *ganas*. 6. On the east end of the chamber is Mahishasuri slaying the buffalo-demon ; a four-armed figure with a club stands in front, and one with sword behind : above are *gandharvas*.

On each side the approach to the shrine is a large sculpture :—1. On the north side Ravana under Kailasa, with five heads and an animal's —possibly a boars'—rising out of the top of his high cap ; Siva and Parvati with their attendants are represented above. 2. On the south Siva and Parvati playing at *chausar*, with Bhringi beyond, resting his chin and hand on his knee. Parvati is attended by females, one plaiting her hair. The dispute between the gamesters is here pretty well represented. Below is the bull, with the usual gambolling *ganas*.

In front of each pilaster of the ante-chamber stands a female *chauri*-bearer with dwarf attendants. The two columns here are of the Elephanta style, or with compressed cushion capitals, but, in place of brackets, they have deep square abaci carved with figures. The door of the shrine is also elaborately carved. On each side it has a gigantic *dvarapala* with wigged dwarf attendant, one of them with a high cap having the prongs of the *trisula* projecting from the top of it, a broad dagger, a sword, and round his loins a cobra.

The shrine contains a square *salunka* with a water-rotted *linga* in it. A wide and lofty *pradakshina* surrounds it.

CAVE XXII—NILAKANTHA

A little further along, a door leads into a court 42 feet square, within which an ascent of three steps leads to a slightly sloping platform on which stands the Nandi Mandapa—a four-doored chamber, partially ruined. On the south side of the court is a low chapel with the *Ashtamatra*, or eight mothers, all four-armed, and the eighth—Brahmi—with three faces. Thirteen steps lead up to the cave, in front of which at each end is a *dvarapala* besmeared with paint. This excavation is 70 feet by 44, including the end chapels and vestibule of the shrine, and 12 feet high. It has four pillars in front, and two on each of the other three sides of the hall,—all square plain shafts with bases and bracket capitals. At each end is a chapel with an altar. On the walls of the vestibule are a few sculptures,—Ganesa, three devis, —one on a crocodile,—and a four-armed Vishnu, or perhaps Kartikeya. In the shrine is a round *salunkha* and a highly polished *linga* still worshipped, and which the local Brahmans pretend to show blueish streaks upon : hence the name Nilakantha—'blue-throated' one of the names of Siva—given to the cave.

Cave XXIII

On a rather higher level is a low cave consisting of a verandah (partly double) with five doors entering into small cells, one of them containing a round *salunkha* and *linga*, with a *Trimurti* on the back wall.

Cave XXIV—Teli-ka-Gana

Below the front of the last is a series of five low cells, known as "the Oilman's mill." They contain some small sculptures of no special interest.

A little to the north, in the course of a torrent, just where it falls over a cliff, a beginning of a cave has been made, but a flaw in the rock seemingly has stopped progress.

Cave XXV—Kumbharwada

The whole front of the Kumbharwada cave which must have been supported by six columns and pilasters, has fallen away. The hall, including recess is 95 feet long, the width about 27 feet, and height 13 feet 10 inches. An image has been placed on a pedestal at the north end, and at the south is a recess with a shrine behind it containing an oblong altar. Between the front of this recess and the pilaster of the front of the cave is a fat male seated on a rich *gadi* or seat, with a bag in his hand.

At the back of the hall are four free-standing and two attached square pillars with moulded bases. The smaller hall behind these measures 57 feet by 23, and has two pillars in the ends and two at the back, with two attached ones dividing it from the vestibule of the shrine, 30 feet by 9. On the ceiling of the vestibule is a figure of Surya—the Sun-God—in his chariot drawn by seven steeds, and a female at each side shooting with a bow. Was this a Sun-temple? In the shrine, 15 feet square, is an oblong altar.

Cave XXVI—Janwasa

The columns of this temple are quite of the Elephanta pattern. It has four in front, and two pilasters; and at the back two with pilasters. At each end of a spacious hall 16 feet 6 inches high is a chapel raised three or four feet above the floor on a moulded base. The total length, including these chapels, is 112 feet, and the depth to the back of the *pradakshina* 67 feet.

In front of each pilaster of the vestibule is a female *chauri*-bearer—her hair carefully crimped—with dwarf attendant. At the shrine door are two large *dvarapalas* one with a flower; and stout attendants, one with a very high cap terminating in a sharp spear-point, with a skull on the right side of it. In the shrine is a large square *salunkha* and *linga*. The *pradakshina* is wide and lofty.

Cave XXVII—The Milkmaid's Cave

This is on the south edge of a ravine that separates it from the last Saiva cave, and over the scarp at the head of which is a fine waterfall after heavy rain. One octagonal pillar and a fragment of another are left in the verandah : it had, perhaps, two more pillars. The back wall of the verandah is pierced for a door and four windows. On this wall are few carvings :—Lakshmi with two male attendants ; Vishnu, four-armed, with club, *chakra*, and rosary ; Siva with cobra and trident ; Brahma, three-faced, with staff, waterpot, and rosary ; and Mahishasuri with the buffalo. In the north end is Varaha with Prithvi, and in the south Narayana on Sesha half finished. Inside is a hall 58 feet by 22, and 11 feet 8½ inches high, beyond which is a vestibule to the shrine, 23 feet by 10 with a raised floor and two short square pillars in front.

In recesses on each side the shrine door are Vaishnava *dvarapalas* and inside is a long oblong altar at the back of the shrine.

It was doubtless a Vaishnava cave, but the style of it says but little for the wealth or influence of the sect in the days when it was executed.

Cave XXVIII

Under the cliff over which the stream falls are the remains of a couple of cells, and a vestibule and shrine with *dvarapalas*—perhaps Vaishnava— at each side of the door. Inside is the base of a square altar, and on the inside of the front wall is an eight-armed Devi with attendants, still worshipped.

Cave XXIX—Sita's Nani, or Dumar Lena

This cave is often compared with Elephanta or Garapuri, to which it bears a striking resemblance, but it is larger and in some respects finer ; it is also, perhaps, later in age. The great hall, including the shrine, is 148 feet wide by 149 deep, and 17 feet 8 inches high, but the excavation extends to about 240 feet from north to south. Two large lions with small elephants under their paws guard the steps which lead into the hall from three sides. Before the west approach is a large circle for the Nandi. The hall is in the form of a cross, the roof supported by twenty-six massive pillars.

In the front aisles on three sides are large sculptures at each end. In the west aisle, south end, is Ravana shaking Kailasa, as usual, and in the north end Bhairava with two victims. In the south verandah there is a large pit opposite the landing: in the west end Siva and Parvati are playing *chausar*; Nandi and the *ganas* are below, Vishnu to the right of them, and Brahma to the left.

In the east end is the marriage, with Gods and Goddesses above. It is thus described by Kalidasa :—

"E'en Brahma came—Creator—Lord of might,—
And Vishnu glowing from the realms of light.

* * *

By Indra led, each World-upholding lord
With folded arms the mighty God adored,—
In humble robes arrayed, the pomp and pride
Of glorious deity were laid aside.

* * *

Around the fire in solemn rite they trod—
The lovely lady and the glorious God;
Like Day and starry Midnight when they meet
In the broad plains at lofty Meru's feet.
Thrice at the bidding of the priest they came
With swimming eyes around the holy flame;
Then at his word the Bride in order due
Into the blazing fire the parched grain threw,
And towards her face the scented smoke she drew,
While softly wreathing o'er her cheek it hung,
And round her ears in flower-like beauty hung.

* * *

'This flame be witness of your wedded life,—
Be just, thou Husband, and be true thou Wife!'
Such was the priestly blessing on the Bride;—
Eager she listened, as the earth when dried
By parching summer suns drinks deeply in
The first soft dropping when the rains begin.
'Look, gentle Uma,' cried her lord, 'afar!
See'st thou the brightness of yon polar star?
Like that unchanging ray thy faith must shine!'
Sobbing she whispered—" Yes, for ever thine."*

* Griffiths's translation of the *Kumara Sambhava*. For fully detailed accounts of these sculptures see my *Elephanta*.

Outside the pilaster to the south of this is a gigantic Devi with round head-dress peaked in front. Above are four *munis* or sages, and below, three females; a bird or goose pulls at ther mantle: may it not be Sarasvati—'Queen of speech'?

To the south of this is a stair descending down to the stream below.

In the north verandah is Siva as Mahayogi, seated on a lotus, with a club in his left hand: the stalk of the lotus, as in Buddha caves, being upheld by Naga-hooded figures with two worshippers behind them. Opposite to this is Siva dancing the *tandava*, with very fat legs: Parvati is seated at his left,—perhaps because this dance is said to be executed by him occasionally for her pleasure.

On the east wall, outside the pilaster, is a tall female figure—a river goddess—standing on a tortoise, with a single female attendant and *gandharvas*. This is in a small court on the north side of the cave, in the east of which is a low cave much silted up, with a large oblong block of stone inside.

The shrine is in the back wing or recess of the cave and is a small square room containing a *linga*-altar with *linga* in it, with four doors, each guarded by a pair of gigantic *dvarapalas*, each holding a flower in his right hand, and with a female attendant also holding a flower. The head-dresses are varied in almost every case. In the south *pradakshina* is a square cell, and through it another is entered with a deep hole in one corner.

Cave XXXI—Chhota Kailasa

A considerable distance intervenes between the last and Chhota Kailasa, which is some way up the face of the hill, and near to the latter is at least one cave* entirely choked up with earth and not cleared out. Chhota Kailasa was ordered by the Hyderabad Government to be cleared out in 1877, but the local officers failed to accomplish the work. It is a curious work, quite

* This cave has been properly conserved since the inauguration of the Archæological Department.

Dravidian in style, and on the general plan of the hall in Kailasa, having a *mandapa* 36 feet 4 inches square, with sixteen pillars, a porch in front about 10 feet square, and a shrine 14½ feet by 11¾. This is situated in an excavated pit 80 feet wide by about 130 feet long, with two side excavations. This is the first in order, though probably the latest in time, of the Jaina excavations, and had it been cleared out in time to be surveyed and described might have yielded important results. On the front are some decidedly Saiva sculptures. It doubtless contains several loose sculptures of the 13th century; one was found dated Saka 1169, or A.D. 1247.

Cave XXXII

Between the last and the Indra Sabha is another cave* probably never finished, but filled with earth up to the capitals of the pillars. The porch as been hewn out entirely on three sides from the rock. The pillars have cushion capitals, and have been carefully chiselled; those of the porch stand on a screen supported by elephants, and with water-jars in compartments as ornamentation. A large portion of the earth in front has been removed, but inside it is left nearly full.

Cave XXXIII—Indra Sabha

The Indra Sabha, so called, is rather the group of Jaina caves than a single cave and its appendages: in reality two double-storied caves and a single one, with their wings and subordinate chapels, etc. The first, however, is pretty well known as the Indra Sabha. The court of it is entered through a screen wall facing the south. Outside this on the east side is a chapel with two pillars in front and two more at the back. The walls are sculptured with Parsvanatha on the north end, nude,—as in all cases in these caves, —with a seven-hooded snake overshadowing him, a female attendant with snake-hood bearing a *chhatri* or umbrella over him; on each side are Hindu divinities, one with grinning face on his stomach, and below at his

* This cave has since been cleaned.

INDRA SABHA: INDRANI

left hand a pair of worshippers. On the south end is Gomata, also nude, with a creeper twining round his limbs, with female attendants and worshippers. Elsewhere we find Mahavira, the last of the Jaina Tirthankaras, or men who by their austerities set themselves free from liability to further transmigration, and so obtained *nirvana*. These figures are remarkably like the figures of Buddha in the meditative attitude with his hands in his lap, only they are usually represented as nude, and have a drummer and other musicians over their heads. On the back wall is a figure, generally known as Indra, under a tree with parrots in it, seated on an elephant and with two attendants; on the right side is Indrani, and in the shrine Mahavira.

Inside the court on the right side there is a large elephant on a pedestal, and on the left stood a fine monolithic column 27 feet 4 inches high, with a quadruple or *chaumukha* image on the top, but it fell over against the rock the day after Lord Northbrook visited the caves. In the centre of the court is a pavilion or *mandapa* over a quadruple image,—either of Rishabhanatha, the first of the twenty-four Tirthankaras, or of Mahavira, the last; the throne is supported by a wheel and lions, as in Bauddha temples.

On the west side of the court is a cave or hall with two pillars in front and four inside. In the central compartment of the south wall is Parsvanatha, the 23rd Tirthankara; and opposite, with deer and a dog at his feet, is Gomata or Gautama, to whom three very colossal images are erected in the Canarese country,—at Belgola, Karkala, and Yenur. In this cave they are only larger than those in the cave outside the gate, and they recur again and again in these caves with only slight variations in the surrounding figures. On the back wall are Indra and Indrani, and in the shrine is Mahavira on a *sinhasana*, with a triple umbrella over his head. Between this and the main cave, but lower, is a small chapel long partially filled up, in which the Indra and Indrani are peculiarly well cut, though recently the face of the latter seems to have been wilfully damaged by some scoundrel. Over this chapel is another similarly furnished, and directly opposite is still another like it.

Entering the lower hall, we find it has a sort of double verandah, divided by a screen, beyond which is a twelve-pillared hall, few of the columns of which, however, have been entirely cut out from the rock, and the aisles are little more than begun. At the left end of the front verandah, on the pilasters, are two colossal nude images of Santinatha, the 16th Tirthankara, with an inscription under that on the right in characters of the 9th or 10th century :—

Sri Sohila brahma-
charinah Santibhatta-
raka pratimeyam.

" The image of Santibhattaraka, (*made by*) Sohila, a Brahmacharin (*i.e.* pandit of the Digambara or naked Jains). "

Beyond this is a chapel with shrine and the usual sculptures. Inside the hall on one of the pillars is another large nude image, with one line underneath :—

Sri Nagavarmma krita pratima,
" The image made by Sri Nagavarmma."

Near the east end of the verandah a stone stair leads to the upper story, and facing the bottom of it is a chapel sculptured much as the rest,—Parsvanatha on the right, Gomata on the left, Indra and Indrani at the back, and Mahavira on the throne in the shrine.

The stair lands in the verandah of the grand hall, once all bright with painting, of which some smoked fragments still remain, especially of the roof. Two pillars of "broken square " pattern, with their pilasters connected by a low wall, support the front ; two others with boldly moulded square bases and sixteen-sided shafts and capitals, with a low partition between, form the back of the verandah, divid-

INDRA SABHA : INDRA

INDRA SABHA : Exterior (*before restoration*)

ing it from the hall; and twelve, of four different patterns, surround the hall inside. Colossal figures of Indra and Indrani, the one under a banyan, the other under a mango-tree, occupy the ends of the verandah, which is 14½ feet high. The walls of the side and back aisles are divided into compartments filled with Jinas or Tirthankaras. The centre space on each end has a large Jina on a *sinhasana ;* one on each side the shrine door is devoted to Parsvanatha and Gomata ; and the others have two Mahaviras each, under different Bo-trees, as with the Buddhas, but between the Bo-trees is a figure holding up a garland, and above him another blowing a conch, while at the outer sides are *gandharvas.* On the pilasters on each side the shrine door is a tall nude guardian and on the next pilaster a squat Mahavira. The door has two slender advanced pillars, beaten by the Brahmin guides to show the reverberation, and called by them the *damru* or drum of the idol. Over and around this door is a mass of carving. The shrine, 12 feet 8 inches high, is, as usual, occupied by Mahavira.

In the centre of the great hall has stood a quadruple image (*chaumukha*), now destroyed, in a sort of *salunkha ;* and, over it on the roof, an immense lotus-flower on a square slab with holes in the four corners and centre, as if for pendent lamps.

A door in the south-east corner leads, through a cell with a sort of trough in the corner of it, and a natural hole in the roof, into a small cave on the east side of the court. The few steps leading down to it occupy a small lobby carved all round with Jinas, etc. This hall has a verandah in front, and inside are four square pillars with round capitals. Gomata occupies a recess on the right, and Parsvanatha another on the left. Indra, with a bag in his left and a cocoanut in his right hand, occupies the south end of the verandah ; while Indrani faces him in the entrance,—in fact much the same places as the supposed patrons occupy in Bauddha caves. Nude Jaina *dvarapalas* guard the entrance of the shrine, which contains the usual image. Some scraps of painting still remain on the roof of this apartment.

Returning through the great hall, a door in the north-west corner leads through a small room into the temple on the west side corresponding to the last described. It has a carefully carved facade, the sculpture still sharp and spirited. In the entrance to it on the right hand is a four-armed Devi with two discs in the upper hands, and a *vajra* in her left on her knee; and on the left another Devi,—perhaps Sarasvati,—eight-armed, with a peacock. The hall is exactly similar in plan to that on the east, but the four central pillars have the looped drooping capitals of the great hall, and everything has been finished in the close-grained rock more elaborately and sharply. Indra, Gomata. and Parsvanatha recur in their usual positions.

Cave XXXIII—Jagannatha Sabha

A little beyond the Indra Sabha is another cave temple with a court in front; the screen, if any, and the *chaumukha mandapa*, however, must have been structural, and have now disappeared; while the number of fragments of loose images that were discovered in cleaning out this cave testify to the quantity of sculpture that must have been in these caves in addition to what was cut in the rock in the original execution of the work.

On the west side of the court is a hall with two heavy square pillars in front, and four in the middle area. It is sculptured like all the rest, Parsvanatha on the left and Gomata on the right, with Mahavira or some other Jina in the shrines, on pilasters, and in a few recesses. Indra occupies the left end of the verandah, and Indrani the right or north end. There are some inscriptions, a few letters of which are legible, on the pillars of this cave They are in the old Canarese character, and belong probably to about A.D. 800.

Right opposite to this is a chapel with a pretty large cell inside: this is carved with the usual figures also. The cave at the back of the court has been long filled with earth, and the sculpture in it is generally in a remarkable state of preservation. In the ends of the front aisle are Indra and Indrani under trees, with attendants, all very sharply cut, and the features as yet but little injured. The front pillars are square and fluted ; those behind the front aisle square below and sixteen-sided above ; and the four in the inner area are square with drooping cared capitals. The shrine has the vestibule entered under a *torana* or ornamental arch. Parsvanatha, Gomata, etc., recur as before.

To the east side of the entrance, and also facing the south, is a chapel with Mahavira or Santinatha on each end, and further back Parsvanatha on the left and Gomata on the right.

On the right of this is the stair leading to the upper story, consisting of a great twelve-pillared hall varying in height from 13 feet 10 inches to 14 feet 6 inches. Two columns in front and as many in the back row have square bases, and round shafts with florid shoulders : the others are square, except the neck and cushion capital, which are round but not well proportioned: all have massive bases. Two more pillars stand on the bench screen-wall that forms the front of the cave. The roof has been painted in large concentric circles, and on the walls Mahavira is sculptured between fifty and sixty times, Parsvanatha perhaps nine or ten times, and over the heads of the Jinas the space has also been painted with more Jinas and their worshippers. Indra and Indrani are on the back wall outside the *dvarapalas*. In the shrine is a Jinendra with four lions on the front of the throne, and a wheel upheld by a dwarf. Over the Jina is a triple umbrella, and dogs and deer lie together at the foot of the throne. A low-doored cell on the right side of the shrine, and a square hole in the floor, were perhaps for concealing objects of value.

A door in the west end of the front aisle enters a low cell the side of which has been cut away in excavating the hall below it. Through a cell in the other end of the front aisle a hole in the wall leads into the west wing of the Indra Sabha.

Cave XXXIII

A little to the west of the preceding is the last cave of the series. The verandah, which had two square columns and pilasters in front, is gone. The front wall is pierced for a door and two windows. Inside, the roof, 9 feet 8 inches high, is supported by four short pillars—square below, with moulded bases, and having a triangular flat shield on each side—a mark of their comparative modernity.

The right side wall has cut into a cell of the west wing, of the Jagannatha Sabha. Indra and Indrani are in compartments on the back wall, and the other figures are repetitions of those in the other Jaina caves. Having been inaccessible till 1876, when the earth that filled it was taken out, most of the sculptures in this cave are comparatively sharp and fresh.

Parsvanatha

Over the top of this spur is a structural building facing W. by N. erected early last century by a Banya of Aurangabad over a gigantic image of Parsvanatha cut in the red trap of this part of the hill. It measures 9 feet from knee to knee, and 10½ feet from the top knot on the underside of the cushion on which it squats, and 16 feet from the snakehoods over his head to the base of the *sinhasana*, which has a wheel in front.

Right and left of him are worshippers among whom are Siva and Bhavani. On the cushion on which he sits is an inscription dated 1234—5 A.D., which is thus rendered by Dr. Buhler :—

Translation

Hail! In the year 1156 of the famous Saka era, in the year (of the Brihaspati cycle) called Jaya.

In Sri (Vardhanapura) was born Ranugi.........his son (*was*) Galugi, (*the latter's wife*) Svarna, (*dear*) to the world.

AHALYA BAI'S TEMPLE: ELLORA

2. From those two sprang four sons, Chakresvara and the rest. Chakresvara was chief among them, excelling through the virtue of liberality.

3. He gave, on the hill that is frequented by Charanas a monument of Parsvanatha, and by (*this act of*) liberality (*he made*) an oblation of his *karma*.*

4. Many huge images of the Lordly Jinas he made, and converted the Charanadri thereby into a holy *tirtha*, just as Bharata (*made* Mount Kailasa (*a tirtha*).

5. The unique image of faith, of firm and pure convictions, kind, constant to his faithful wife, resembling the tree of paradise (*in liberality*), Chakresvara becomes a protector of the pure faith, a fifth Vasudeva. *Quod felix faustumque sit!* Phalguna 8, Wednesday.

Below this, on the slope of the spur are several small caves, all Jaina, but now much ruined; and near the summit is a plain cave with two square columns in front.

* i.e. destroyed his *karma*, which bound him to the Samsara.